EXPLORING OUR UNIVERSE

THE MOON

KELLY DOUDNA

Checkerboard Library

An Imprint of Abdo Publishing
abdopublishing.com

abdopublishing.com

Published by Abdo Publishing, a division of ABDO, PO Box 398166, Minneapolis, Minnesota 55439.
Printed in the United States of America, North Mankato, Minnesota
102016
012017

THIS BOOK CONTAINS RECYCLED MATERIALS

Design: Emily O'Malley, Mighty Media, Inc.
Production: Mighty Media, Inc.
Editor: Paige Polinsky
Cover Photograph: NASA
Interior Photographs: NASA, pp. 5, 7, 11, 12, 13, 15, 18, 19, 21, 22, 23, 25, 26, 29; Shutterstock, p. 9

Publisher's Cataloging-in-Publication Data

Names: Doudna, Kelly, author.
Title: The moon / by Kelly Doudna.
Description: Minneapolis, MN : Abdo Publishing, 2017. | Series: Exploring our universe | Includes bibliographical references and index.
Identifiers: LCCN 2016944825 | ISBN 9781680784053 (lib. bdg.) | ISBN 9781680797589 (ebook)
Subjects: LCSH: Moon--Juvenile literature.
Classification: DDC 523.3--dc23
LC record available at http://lccn.loc.gov/2016944825

CONTENTS

MISSION THE MOON

The moon is Earth's closest celestial companion. Yet it is the only moon without a specific name! This is because ancient astronomers didn't know other moons existed.

THE ORIGINAL CALENDAR

For thousands of years, the moon has been an important timekeeper. As it orbits Earth, different parts of the moon are visible. Its cycle is the basis for our modern calendar. Time can be marked by the moon's changing appearance.

A CLOSER LOOK

Italian astronomer Galileo Galilei made the first scientific observations of the moon. He studied it through one of the earliest telescopes. Galileo saw that the moon's light and dark areas were really mountains and craters.

The moon, seen here from the International Space Station, is Earth's nearest neighbor. But it is still about 238,855 miles (384,400 km) away!

HOUSTON, WE HAVE LIFTOFF

Today, we know much more about our moon. Astronauts and **probes** have studied it from every side. Observing our moon is one way we can learn more about our universe.

CHAPTER 1

ONE OF A KIND

The moon is Earth's only natural satellite. It is also the brightest object in the sky after the sun. But the moon doesn't produce its own light. Instead, it reflects the sun's light. Though the moon appears white, its surface is gray.

The moon rotates around its axis, just as Earth does. One rotation of the moon takes about 27 days. In that time, the moon also completes one orbit around Earth. As the moon travels, its same side always faces Earth. This is known as being tidally locked.

Earth's gravitational pull drags the moon into Earth's orbit. But the moon has gravitational pull too. While orbiting Earth, the moon pulls Earth's water slightly toward it. This creates ocean tides. High and low tides occur as Earth spins and faces the moon at different angles.

Our moon orbits Earth at a speed of 2,288 miles per hour (3,683 kmh). The US spacecraft *Galileo* took this photo from 3.9 million miles (6.2 million km) away.

CHAPTER 2

MANY FACES

The sun always lights the half of the moon that faces it. But the Earth, moon, and sun are always moving. Their positions determine what the moon looks like from Earth.

A full moon occurs when the moon and sun are on opposite sides of Earth. The moon's entire sunlit side faces

THE MOON'S PHASES

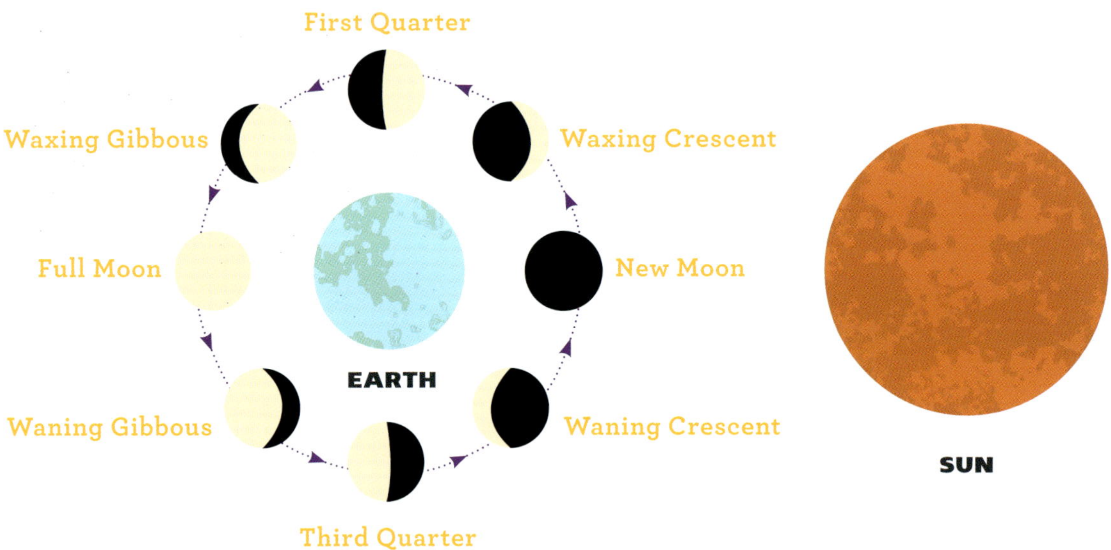

September's full moon is called the harvest moon. Its brightness helps farmers gather their crops through the night.

Earth. A new moon occurs when the moon and sun are on the same side of Earth. The entire unlit side faces Earth. The moon is not visible to observers on Earth. The moon's in-between phases also have names. A crescent moon is less full than a gibbous moon.

CHAPTER 3

MAKING THE MOON

Scientists aren't certain how the moon came to be. But many support the Giant Impact **Hypothesis**. According to this theory, Earth began to form about 4.5 billion years ago. Another forming planet, Theia, orbited nearby.

Theia eventually **collided** with Earth and shattered. Most of its outer material shot into orbit. The Earth also lost some of its crust and **mantle**, but not as much as Theia.

Gravity recombined Theia's heavier pieces into one large body. This became Earth. Debris began to orbit Earth, including Theia's leftover **core**. The debris combined around the core and became the moon.

DID YOU KNOW?

Mercury and Venus don't have any moons. Jupiter has the most moons with 67.

An illustration of the Giant Impact Hypothesis. This hypothesis is also known as the Big Splash Theory.

Some scientists think two early moons formed from Theia's debris. The smaller one **collided** with the larger. They combined to become one moon. Whether there was one early moon or two, the result was the moon of today.

CHAPTER 4

A LITTLE ATMOSPHERE

For a long time, little was known about the moon's atmosphere. But in 1969, the National Aeronautics and Space Administration (**NASA**) began sending men to the moon. These Apollo missions collected much information. In 1972, Apollo 17 astronauts Harrison Schmitt and Eugene Cernan gathered **lunar** rock and atmospheric samples.

The samples contained **helium**, **argon**, and other elements. These elements may have come from solar winds and crashing comets. Some may have escaped the moon's interior.

The moon still has footprints from the astronauts who walked there in the 1960s!

TOOLS OF DISCOVERY

MOON MISSIONS

Until the 1950s, we could only observe the moon from Earth. But in 1959, Russia sent the probe Luna 2 into space. Luna 2 became the first man-made object to land on the moon. And in 1966, Luna 9 took the first photos on the lunar surface.

Later, in 1969, the United States made space history. NASA's Apollo 11 mission landed the first humans on the moon. US astronauts Neil Armstrong and Edwin "Buzz" Aldrin collected rock and soil samples. Five other manned lunar missions later followed.

Apollo 11 launched from the Cape Canaveral Air Force Station in Florida. The mission lasted eight days.

An object's gravity is determined by its size and mass. The moon is smaller than Earth. It is also less **dense**. That means the moon's gravity is much weaker than Earth's. But it's still strong enough to keep rocks, boulders, and astronauts from floating away.

Humans need gravity equal to at least 15 percent of Earth's. Without it, we can't determine up from down. The moon has just enough gravity at 17 percent. Even so, moonwalking astronauts sometimes have trouble staying on their feet!

The moon's gravity is not just weak. It's irregular. Scientists have found areas of higher gravity around large craters. This unevenness has disrupted the orbits of **probes** exploring the moon.

DID YOU KNOW?

The moon's atmosphere is very thin. There is no wind or turbulence like the air on Earth. So the moon's surface remains largely undisturbed.

The Apollo space suits weighed about 280 pounds (127 kg). But low gravity made it easy for the astronauts to bounce around while wearing them.

CHAPTER 5

MAKEUP OF THE MOON

The moon's structure is very similar to that of Earth. According to the Giant Impact **Hypothesis**, Earth and Theia also had similar makeups. Because the moon formed from the Earth-Theia **collision**, it inherited their qualities. Like the Earth, the moon has a **core**, a **mantle**, and a crust.

The similarities don't end there. While the Earth has earthquakes, the moon has moonquakes! In the early 1970s, **NASA** astronauts left **seismic** sensors on the moon's surface. Researchers studied these quakes to learn more about the moon's core. In 2011, this data revealed that a hot, liquid outer core surrounds the moon's solid inner core. Both cores contain mostly **iron**.

DID YOU KNOW?

Our moon is the second-densest in the solar system. Jupiter's moon Io is denser.

LAYERS OF THE MOON

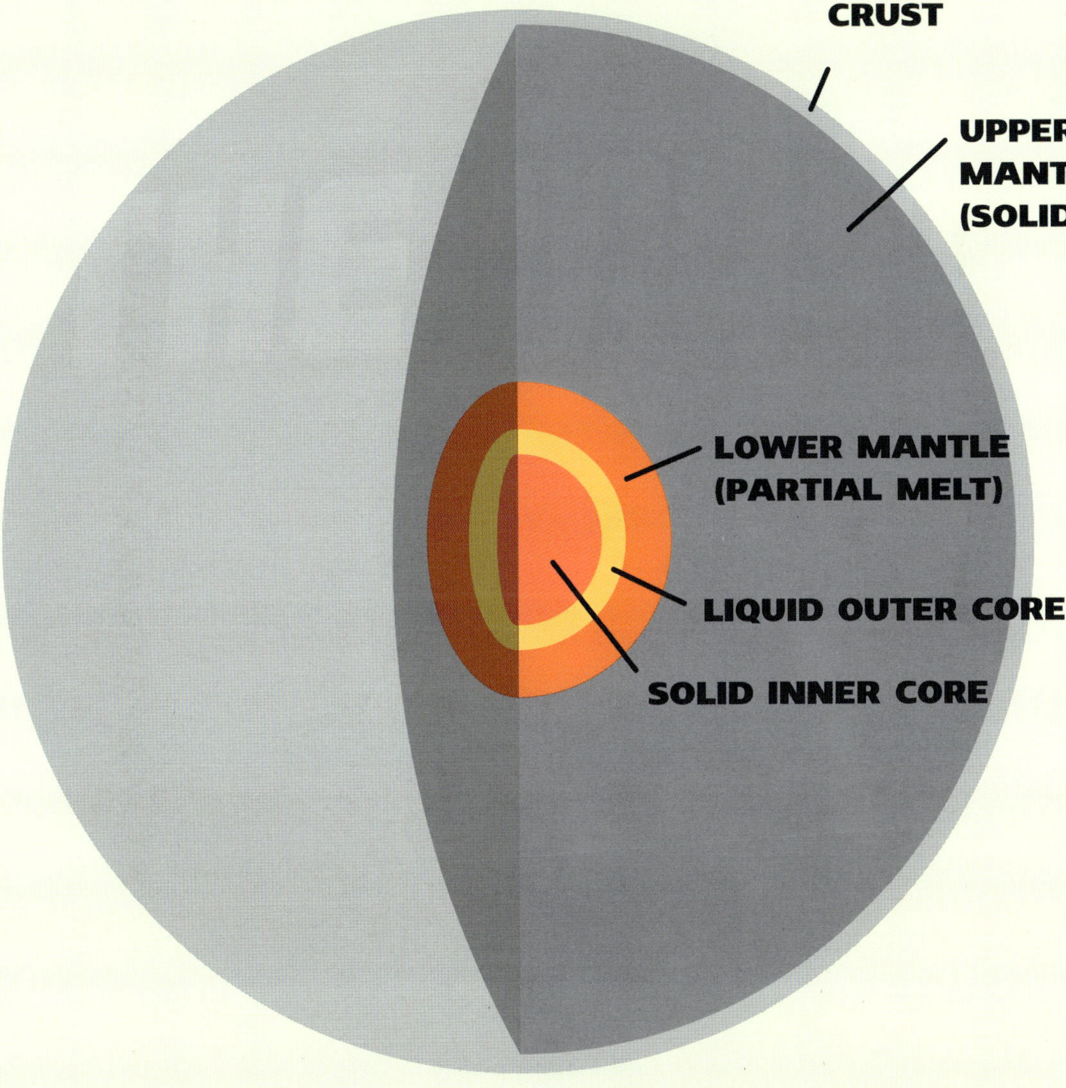

In 2009, scientists discovered moon rocks containing pink spinel. Pure forms of this mineral are used as gemstones on Earth.

Like the **core**, the moon's **mantle** has two parts. The lower mantle, or asthenosphere, is not completely liquid. But it is hot enough that its material can flow. The upper mantle is called the lithosphere. It is completely solid. It formed when the young moon's molten **lava** cooled and hardened.

The moon's crust is called the regolith. The solid regolith is similar to concrete. For billions of years, asteroids and meteoroids have crashed into its surface. This has created a layer of fine dust on top of the regolith.

SUPER SCIENTIST

HARRISON SCHMITT

Geologist Harrison Schmitt was the first professional scientist to visit the moon. In 1965, NASA chose Schmitt for its scientist-astronaut program. In 1972, Schmitt joined the Apollo 17 mission. Schmitt and crewmate Eugene Cernan were the last people to visit the moon.

Schmitt collected important samples from the moon's surface. One sample was called orange soil. This turned out to be tiny beads of volcanic glass. Studies later found traces of water in these beads. This suggests there was once water on the moon.

Schmitt was the first crew member to see the orange soil. He discovered it by scuffing the moon's surface with his boot.

CHAPTER 6

THE MAN IN THE MOON

Sometimes it looks like the moon has a face. But this is a trick of the light. The dark areas, or maria, are the moon's lowest elevation points. They were created when meteors crashed into the young moon's surface.

The meteor crashes broke through the moon's crust. Molten **lava** oozed to the surface and hardened. The hardened lava is less reflective than the moon's regolith. So, it appears darker.

People from different locations see different shapes in the moon's maria. In the northern half of the world, many people think the moon looks like a man's face.

In the 1960s, the *Lunar Orbiter 2* spacecraft photographed the moon's craters. This photograph was one of the first close-up images of the moon's landscape.

The moon's light areas, or terrae, have high elevations. They are covered with dusty meteor craters. The dust reflects sunlight. So, it appears lighter.

CHAPTER 7

THE FAR SIDE

One side of the moon never faces Earth. People often call this the dark side. But it doesn't spend any less time in the sunlight. The name *far side* is more **accurate**.

Nobody knew what the far side looked like until 1959. That year, Russian **probe** Luna 3 took the first photos from orbit. And nearly ten years later, we got even closer.

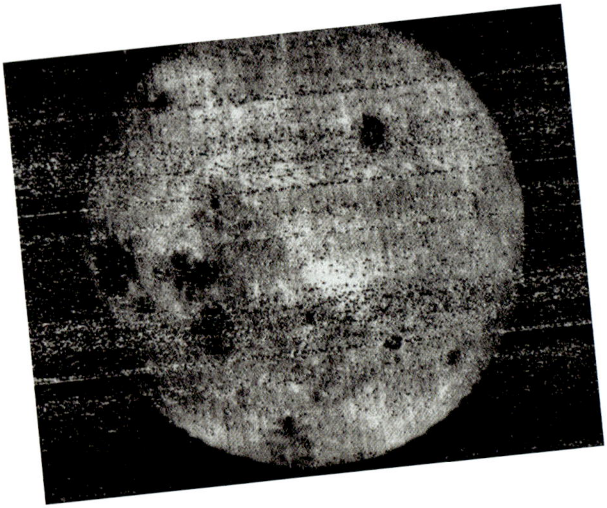

Luna 3 sent 17 far-side photographs back to Earth. These images gave us a whole new look at the moon.

In 2011, the Clementine mission captured a clear photo of the moon's far side. The crust on this side is much thicker than on the near side.

No manned missions have ever landed on the far side. But in 1968, the Apollo 8 astronauts became the first to view it from orbit. We now know that there are few maria there. Most of its surface is covered in impact craters.

CHAPTER 8

ECLIPSES

LUNAR ECLIPSE

At least two **lunar** eclipses occur each year. During an eclipse, Earth is between the full moon and the sun. Earth casts its shadow, or umbra, on the moon.

Perfect **alignment** creates a total lunar eclipse. Earth's full shadow falls on the moon. Sunlight bends around Earth's atmosphere, making the moon appear red. A partial lunar eclipse occurs when Earth's alignment is not perfect. Then, only a portion of Earth's umbra covers the moon.

SOLAR ECLIPSE

Each year brings between two and five solar eclipses. A solar eclipse occurs during a new moon. Then, the moon is between the Earth and the sun. Sometimes, the moon completely covers the sun. This is a total solar eclipse.

Earth's umbra covers the moon in a total lunar eclipse.

Total solar eclipses are spectacular. The moon's black disk covers all but the sun's outer atmosphere, or corona. The corona sometimes looks like bright flames.

An annular solar eclipse creates a beautiful ring of fire. But it is unsafe to view without proper safety equipment.

A partial solar eclipse occurs when the moon's **alignment** is imperfect. Some of the sun remains visible. It is unsafe to look directly at a partial solar eclipse.

During an annular solar eclipse, the moon is farther away from Earth. Its alignment is perfect, just like a total eclipse. But the moon doesn't cover the sun completely. The sun's edge and corona remain visible. A solid, bright ring can be seen around the dark moon.

The moon and its changing appearance is our constant companion. But there is still much we don't know about it. Today, scientists continue to study the moon. Their **satellites** and **probes** continue to gather **lunar** data. By studying this information, we can learn more about space through our nearest celestial neighbor.

DID YOU KNOW?

The sun is about 400 times wider than the moon. But the moon is about 400 times closer to Earth. That's why the sun and moon often look the same size in the sky.

LUNAR GUIDEBOOK

Age

- 4.5 billion years

Other Names

- Luna or Selene, after the Roman and Greek goddesses of the moon

Primary Planet

- Earth

Main Elements

- Oxygen, silicon, magnesium, **iron**, calcium, and aluminum

Size

- 2,159 miles (3,474 km) wide

Distance to Earth

- 238,855 miles (384,400 km)

Rotation

- 27.3 Earth days

Speed of Orbit

- 2,288 miles per hour (3,683 kmh)

Hottest Surface Temperature

- 253 degrees Fahrenheit (122.8°C)

Coldest Surface Temperature

- –387 degrees Fahrenheit (–232.8°C)

Early astronomers thought the moon's dark areas looked like oceans. They called them maria, after the Latin word *mare* for sea.

GLOSSARY

accurate — free from error.

alignment — arrangement in a straight line.

argon — a colorless gas used in various products, such as lasers and some light bulbs.

collide — to come together with force. An act or instance of colliding is a collision.

core — the central part of a celestial body, usually having different physical properties from the surrounding parts.

dense — thick or compact.

helium — a light, colorless gas that does not burn.

hypothesis (heye-PAH-thus-suhs) — an unproven idea or theory based on known facts that leads to further study.

iron — a type of metal that rusts in moist air.

lava — the hot, liquid rock that pours out of a volcano when it erupts.

lunar — of or relating to the moon.

mantle — the part of a planet between the crust and the core.

NASA — National Aeronautics and Space Administration. NASA is a US government agency that manages the nation's space program and conducts flight research.

probe — device used to explore and send back information.

satellite — An object, either natural or manufactured, that orbits a larger heavenly body. A manufactured satellite relays scientific information back to Earth.

seismic — of or relating to vibrations in a celestial body.

WEBSITES

To learn more about Exploring Our Universe, visit booklinks.abdopublishing.com. These links are routinely monitored and updated to provide the most current information available.

INDEX